PETER MAYLE

POSTCARDS FROM
SUMMER

PENGUIN BOOKS

PENGUIN BOOKS

Published by the Penguin Group. Penguin Books Ltd, 27 Wrights Lane, London w8 5TZ, England. Penguin Books USA Inc., 375 Hudson Street, New York, New York 10014, USA. Penguin Books Australia Ltd, Ringwood, Victoria, Australia. Penguin Books Canada Ltd, 10 Alcorn Avenue, Toronto, Ontario, Canada M4V 3B2. Penguin Books (NZ) Ltd, 182–190 Wairau Road, Auckland 10, New Zealand · Penguin Books Ltd, Registered Offices: Harmondsworth, Middlesex, England · This extract is from *Toujours Provence*, by Peter Mayle, first published by Hamish Hamilton 1991. This edition published in Penguin Books 1996 · Copyright © Peter Mayle, 1991. All rights reserved · The moral right of the author has been asserted · Typeset by Rowland Phototypesetting Ltd, Bury St Edmunds, Suffolk. Printed in England by Clays Ltd, St Ives plc · Except in the United States of America, this book is sold subject to the condition that it shall not, by way of trade or otherwise, be lent, re-sold, hired out, or otherwise circulated without the publisher's prior consent in any form of binding or cover other than that in which it is published and without a similar condition including this condition being imposed on the subsequent purchaser · 10 9 8 7 6 5 4 3 2 1

Postcards from Summer

It has taken us three years to accept the fact that
we live in the same house, but in two different
places.

What we think of as normal life starts in
September. Apart from market days in the
towns, there are no crowds. Traffic on the back
roads is sparse during the day – a tractor, a
few vans – and virtually non-existent at night.
There is always a table in every restaurant,
except perhaps for Sunday lunch. Social life is
intermittent and uncomplicated. The baker has
bread, the plumber has time for a chat, the
postman has time for a drink. After the first
deafening weekend of the hunting season, the
forest is quiet. Each field has a stooped, reflec-
tive figure working among the vines, very
slowly up one line, very slowly down the next.
The hours between noon and two are dead.

And then we come to July and August.

We used to treat them as just another two

months of the year; hot months, certainly, but nothing that required much adjustment on our part except to make sure that the afternoon included a siesta.

We were wrong. Where we live in July and August is still the Lubéron, but it's not the same Lubéron. It is the Lubéron *en vacances*, and our past efforts to live normally during abnormal times have been miserably unsuccessful. So unsuccessful that we once considered cancelling summer altogether and going somewhere grey and cool and peaceful, like the Hebrides.

But if we did, we would probably miss it, all of it, even the days and incidents that have reduced us to sweating, irritated, over-tired zombies. So we have decided to come to terms with the Lubéron in the summer, to do our best to join the rest of the world on holiday and, like them, to send postcards telling distant friends about the wonderful times we are having. Here are a few.

MARIGNANE AIRPORT

Three in the afternoon, and still no sign of the one o'clock plane.

When I called to confirm that it was on time, I was given the standard optimistic lie. And so I left home at 11.30 and spent the hottest hour of a hot day on the *autoroute*, trying to avoid sudden death among a swarm of Renault 5 missiles launched early that morning from Paris and targeted on the Côte d'Azur. How can these people steer with all four wheels off the ground?

Un petit retard is indicated on the flight arrivals board, nothing much, forty-five minutes. Time for coffee, two coffees. The flights to Oran have been delayed too, and the airport lounge is carpeted with Arab workmen and their families going home, the children nesting among overstuffed plastic suitcases striped in blue and pink and white. The expressions on the dark, seamed faces of the men are patient and resigned.

The girl at the desk answers my question about the flight by pointing at the board: forty-five minutes late. When I say that the plane is already an hour late, she shrugs and consults the crystal ball in her computer. Yes, it is as the board indicates, forty-five minutes late. Has the plane left London yet? Yes, she says. But I know she's been trained in deception like all the rest of them.

It is just before five when the plane gets in and the pale-faced, bad-tempered passengers begin to come through. The first hours of their holiday have been spent sitting on the tarmac at Heathrow. Some of them make the mistake of slapping their passports down impatiently on the counter in front of the immigration officer. He takes his revenge by examining each page with painstaking, exasperating thoroughness, pausing between pages to lick the tip of his finger.

My friends come through, looking rumpled but cheerful. A few minutes to pick up the bags and then we can be back in plenty of time for a swim before dinner. But a quarter of an hour later they are still waiting in the deserted baggage claim area. The airline has made separate holiday arrangements for one of their suitcases

– Newcastle, Hong Kong, who knows? – and we join the other castaways in Lost Luggage.

We are home by 7.30, almost exactly eight hours after I left.

SAINT-TROPEZ

Cherchez les nudistes! It is open season for nature-lovers, and there is likely to be a sharp increase in the number of applicants wishing to join the Saint-Tropez police force.

The mayor, Monsieur Spada, has decreed that in the name of safety and hygiene there will be no more naked sunbathing on the public beaches. '*Le nudisme intégral est interdit*,' says Monsieur Spada, and he has empowered the police to seize and arrest any offenders. Well, perhaps not to seize them, but to track them down and fine them 75 francs, or as much as 1,500 francs if they have been guilty of creating a public outrage. Exactly where a nudist might keep 1,500 francs is a question that is puzzling local residents.

Meanwhile, a defiant group of nudists has

5

set up headquarters in some rocks behind *la plage de la Moutte*. A spokeswoman for the group has said that under no circumstances would bathing suits be worn. Wish you were here.

THE MELON FIELD

Faustin's brother Jacky, a wiry little man of sixty or so, grows melons in the field opposite the house. It's a large field, but he does all the work himself, and by hand. In the spring I have often seen him out there for six or seven hours, back bent like a hinge, his hoe chopping at the weeds that threaten to strangle his crop. He doesn't spray – who would eat a melon tasting of chemicals? – and I think he must enjoy looking after his land in the traditional way.

Now that the melons are ripening, he comes to the field at six every morning to pick the ones that are ready. He takes them up to Ménerbes to be packed in shallow wooden crates. From Ménerbes they go to Cavaillon, and from Cavaillon to Avignon, to Paris, everywhere. It amuses Jacky to think of people in smart restaurants paying *une petite fortune* for a simple thing like a melon.

If I get up early enough I can catch him before he goes to Ménerbes. He always has a couple of melons that are too ripe to travel, and he sells them to me for a few francs.

As I walk back to the house, the sun clears the top of the mountain and it is suddenly hot on my face. The melons, heavy and satisfying in my hands, are still cool from the night air. We have them for breakfast, fresh and sweet, less than ten minutes after they have been picked.

BEHIND THE BAR

There is a point at which a swimming pool ceases to be a luxury and becomes very close to a necessity, and that point is when the temperature hits 100 degrees. Whenever people ask us about renting a house for the summer, we always tell them this, and some of them listen.

Others don't, and within two days of arriving

they are on the phone telling us what we told them months before. It's so *hot*, they say. Too hot for tennis, too hot for cycling, too hot for sightseeing, too hot, too hot. Oh for a pool. You're so lucky.

There is a hopeful pause. Is it my imagination, or can I actually hear the drops of perspiration falling like summer rain on the pages of the telephone directory?

I suppose the answer is to be callous but helpful. There is a public swimming pool near Apt, if you don't mind sharing the water with a few hundred small brown dervishes on their school holidays. There is the Mediterranean, only an hour's drive away; no, with traffic it could take two hours. Make sure you have some bottles of Évian in the car. It wouldn't do to get dehydrated.

Or you could close the shutters against the sun, spend the day in the house and spring forth refreshed into the evening air. It would be difficult to acquire the souvenir suntan, but at least there would be no chance of heatstroke.

These brutal and unworthy suggestions barely have time to cross my mind before the

voice of despair turns into the voice of relief.
Of course! We could come over in the morning for a quick dip without disturbing you.
Just a splash. You won't even know we've been.

They come at noon, with friends. They swim. They take the sun. Thirst creeps up on them, much to their surprise, and that's why I'm behind the bar. My wife is in the kitchen, making lunch for six. *Vivent les vacances.*

THE NIGHT WALK

The dogs cope with the heat by sleeping through it, stretched out in the courtyard or curled in the shade of the rosemary hedge. They come to life as the pink in the sky is turning to darkness, sniffing the breeze, jostling each other around our feet in their anticipation of a walk. We take the torch and follow them into the forest.

It smells of warm pine needles and baked earth, dry and spicy when we step on a patch of thyme. Small, invisible creatures slither away from us and rustle through the leaves of the wild box that grows like a weed.

Sounds carry: *cigales* and frogs, the muffled thump of music through the open window of a faraway house, the clinks and murmurs of dinner drifting up from Faustin's terrace. The hills on the other side of the valley, uninhabited for ten months a year, are pricked with lights that will be switched off at the end of August.

We get back to the house and take off our shoes, and the warmth of the flagstones is an invitation to swim. A dive into dark water, and then a last glass of wine. The sky is clear except for a jumble of stars; it will be hot again tomorrow. Hot and slow, just like today.

A SLIGHT MECHANICAL PROBLEM

Our friend had decided to trade in her old car for a new one, and the young car salesman was determined to give her the benefit of his sales pitch. Dapper in a suit despite the heat, he pranced around the new car, pointing out its various attractions with elaborate flourishes, shooting his cuffs and rattling his jewellery.

Our friend endured this with as much patience as she could summon up, and then suggested that a test drive might be a practical way of judging the car's many virtues.

Of course, said the salesman, *mais attention!* He removed his sunglasses for emphasis. This model is very much more *nerveuse* than yours. When I drove it here today, even I was impressed. One touch on the accelerator and you are flying. You will see.

After much meticulous adjustment of the driving position and a final warning about the incredible velocity that was waiting to be unleashed, our friend was presented with the ignition key.

The engine coughed once, and died. Second and third attempts were no more successful. The smile on the salesman's face faded. The car obviously needed a man's touch. He took over in the driving seat and failed to start the car. *Incroyable!* What can be the problem? He opened the bonnet and looked at the engine. He burrowed under the dashboard searching for a loose connection.

Was it at all possible, our friend asked, that the car needed petrol? The salesman tried to hide the scorn he felt for empty-headed women who ask such ridiculous questions, but to humour her turned the key again and inspected the fuel gauge. Drier than dry. He flounced out of the car. Unfortunately, as this was a small showroom and not a garage, petrol was not available on the premises. Another rendezvous would have to be arranged for the test drive. Could Madame come back this afternoon? No? *Merde*.

The desire to conclude the sale overcame the heat and the loss of face, and the young man in the dapper suit had to walk half a mile up the N100 to borrow a jerrican of petrol from the nearest garage, leaving our friend in charge of the showroom. She made a joke about bringing her own petrol next time she wanted to buy a car, which was not well received.

I had been cutting lavender with a pair of secateurs and I was making a slow, amateurish job
of it, nearly an hour to do fewer than a dozen
clumps. When Henriette arrived at the house
with a basket of aubergines, I was pleased to
have the chance to stop.

Henriette looked at the lavender, looked at
the secateurs and shook her head at the ignor-
ance of her neighbour. Didn't I know how to
cut lavender? What was I doing with those secateurs? Where was my *faucille*?

She went to her van and came back with a
blackened sickle, its needle tip embedded in an
old wine cork for safety. It was surprisingly
light, and felt sharp enough to shave with. I
made a few passes with it in the air, and Henriette shook her head again. Obviously, I needed
a lesson.

She hitched up her skirt and attacked the
nearest row of lavender, gathering the long
stems into a tight bunch with one arm and
slicing them off at the bottom with a single 13

smooth pull of the sickle. In five minutes she had cut more than I had in an hour. It looked easy; bend, gather, pull. Nothing to it.

'*Voilà!*' said Henriette. 'When I was a little girl in the Basses Alpes, we had hectares of lavender, and no machines. Everyone used the *faucille.*'

She passed it back to me, told me to mind my legs and went off to join Faustin in the vines.

It wasn't as easy as it looked, and my first effort produced a ragged, uneven clump, more chewed than sliced. I realized that the sickle was made for right-handed lavender cutters, and I had to compensate for being left-handed by slicing away from me. My wife came out to tell me to mind my legs. She doesn't trust me with sharp implements, and so she was reassured to see me cutting away from the body. Even with my genius for self-inflicted wounds there seemed to be little risk of amputation.

I had just come to the final clump when Henriette came back. I looked up, hoping for praise, and sliced my index finger nearly through to the bone. There was a great deal of blood, and Henriette asked me if I was giving myself a manicure. I sometimes wonder about her sense of humour. Two days later, she gave me a sickle of my very own, and told me that I was forbidden to use it unless I was wearing gloves.

THE ALCOHOLIC TENDENCIES
OF WASPS

The Provençal wasp, although small, has an evil sting. He also has an ungallant, hit-and-run method of attack in the swimming pool. He paddles up behind his unsuspecting victim, waits until an arm is raised and – *tok!* – strikes deep into the armpit. It hurts for several hours, and often causes people who have been stung to dress in protective clothing before they go swimming. This is the local version of the Miss Wet T-shirt contest.

I don't know whether all wasps like water, but here they love it – floating in the shallow end, dozing in the puddles on the flagstones, keeping an eye out for the unguarded armpit 15 and the tender extremity – and after one disastrous day during which not only armpits but inner thighs received direct hits (obviously, some wasps can hold their breath and operate under water), I was sent off to look for wasp traps.

When I found them, in a *droguerie* in the back alleys of Cavaillon, I was lucky enough to find a wasp expert behind the counter. He demonstrated for me the latest model in traps, a plastic descendant of the old glass hanging traps that can sometimes be found in flea markets. It had been specially designed, he said, for use around swimming pools, and could be made irresistible to wasps.

It was in two parts. The base was a round bowl, raised off the ground by three flat supports, with a funnel leading up from the bottom. The top fitted over the lower bowl and prevented wasps who had made their way up the funnel from escaping.

But that, said the wasp expert, was the simple part. More difficult, more subtle, more artistic, was the bait. How does one persuade the wasp to abandon the pleasures of the flesh and climb up the funnel into the trap? What could tempt him away from the pool?

After spending some time in Provence, you learn to expect a brief lecture with every purchase, from an organically grown cabbage (two minutes) to a bed (half an hour or more, depending on the state of your back). For wasp traps, you should allow between ten and fifteen minutes. I sat back on the stool in front of the counter and listened.

Wasps, it turned out, like alcohol. Some wasps like it *sucré*, others like it fruity, and there are even those who will crawl anywhere for a drop of *anis*. It is, said the expert, a matter of experimentation, a balancing of flavours and consistencies until one finds the blend that suits the palate of the local wasp population.

He suggested a few basic recipes: sweet vermouth with honey and water, diluted *crème de cassis*, dark beer spiked with *marc*, neat *pastis*. As an added inducement, the funnel can be lightly coated with honey, and a small puddle of water should always be left immediately beneath the funnel.

The expert set up a trap on the counter, and 17

with two fingers imitated a wasp out for a stroll.

He stops, attracted by the puddle of water. The fingers stopped. He approaches the water, and then he becomes aware of something delicious above him. He climbs up the funnel to investigate, he jumps into his cocktail, *et voilà!* – he is unable to get out, being too drunk to crawl back down the funnel. He dies, but he dies happy.

I bought two traps, and tried out the recipes. All of them worked, which leads me to believe that the wasp has a serious drinking problem. And now, if ever a guest is overcome by strong waters, he is described as being as pissed as a wasp.

MALADIE DU LUBÉRON

Most of the seasonal ailments of summer, while they may be uncomfortable or painful or merely embarrassing, are at least regarded with some sympathy. A man convalescing after an explosive encounter with one *merguez* sausage too many is not expected to venture back into polite society until his constitution has recovered. The same is true of third-degree sunburn, *rosé* poisoning, scorpion bites, a surfeit of garlic or the giddiness and nausea caused by prolonged exposure to French bureaucracy. One suffers, but one is allowed to suffer alone and in peace.

There is another affliction, worse than scorpions or rogue sausages, which we have experienced ourselves and seen many times in other permanent residents of this quiet corner of France. Symptoms usually appear some time around mid-July and persist until early September: glazed and bloodshot eyes, yawning, loss of appetite, shortness of temper, lethargy and a mild form of paranoia which manifests itself in sudden urges to join a monastery.

This is the *maladie du Lubéron*, or creeping social fatigue, and it provokes about the same degree of sympathy as a millionaire's servant problems.

If we examine the patients – the permanent residents – we can see why it happens. Permanent residents have their work, their local friends, their unhurried routines. They made a deliberate choice to live in the Lubéron instead of one of the cocktail capitals of the world because they wanted, if not to get away from it all, to get away from most of it. This eccentricity is understood and tolerated for ten months a year.

Try to explain that in July and August. Here come the visitors, fresh from the plane or hot off the *autoroute*, panting for social action. Let's meet some of the locals! To hell with the book in the hammock and the walk in the woods. To hell with solitude; they want people – people for lunch, people for drinks, people for dinner – and so invitations and counter-invitations fly back and forth until every day for weeks has its own social highlight.

As the holiday comes to an end with one final multi-bottle dinner, it is possible to see even on the visitors' faces some traces of weariness. They had no idea it was so lively down here. They are only half-joking when they say they're going to need a rest to get over the whirl of the past few days. Is it always like this? How do you keep it up?

20   It isn't, and we don't. Like many of our

friends, we collapse in between visitations, guarding empty days and free evenings, eating little and drinking less, going to bed early. And every year, when the dust has settled, we talk to other members of the distressed residents' association about ways of making summer less of an endurance test.

We all agree that firmness is the answer. Say no more often than yes. Harden the heart against the surprise visitor who cannot find an hotel room, the deprived child who has no swimming pool, the desperate traveller who has lost his wallet. Be firm; be helpful, be kind, be rude, but above all *be firm*.

And yet I know – I think we all know – that next summer will be the same. I suppose we must enjoy it. Or we would, if we weren't exhausted.

PLACE DU VILLAGE

Cars have been banned from the village square, and stalls or trestle tables have been set up on three sides. On the fourth, a framework of scaffolding, blinking with coloured lights, supports a raised platform made from wooden planks. Outside the café, the usual single row of tables and chairs has been multiplied by ten, and an extra waiter has been taken on to serve the sprawl of customers stretching from the butcher's down to the post office. Children and dogs chase each other through the crowd, stealing lumps of sugar from the tables and dodging the old men's sticks that are waved in mock anger. Nobody will go to bed early tonight, not even the children, because this is the village's annual party, the *fête votive*..

It begins in the late afternoon with a *pot d'amitié* in the square and the official opening of the stalls. Local artisans, the men's faces shining from an afternoon shave, stand behind their tables, glass in hand, or make final adjustments to their displays. There is pottery and jewellery, honey and lavender essence, handwoven fabrics, iron and stone artefacts, paintings and wood carvings, books, postcards, tooled leatherwork, corkscrews with twisted olive-wood handles, patterned sachets of dried herbs. The woman selling pizza does brisk business as the first glass of wine begins to make the crowd hungry.

People drift off, eat, drift back. The night comes down, warm and still, the mountains in the distance just visible as deep black humps against the sky. The three-man accordion band tunes up on the platform and launches into the first of many *paso dobles* while the rock group from Avignon that will follow later rehearses on beer and *pastis* in the café.

The first dancers appear – an old man and his granddaughter, her nose pressed into his belt buckle, her feet balanced precariously on his feet. They are joined by a mother, father and daughter dancing *à trois*, and then by several elderly couples, holding each other with stiff formality, their faces set with concentration as they try to retrace the steps they learned fifty years ago.

The *paso doble* session comes to an end with a flourish and a ruffle of accordion and drums, and the rock group warms up with five minutes of electronic tweaks that bounce off the old stone walls of the church opposite the platform.

The group's singer, a well-built young lady

in tight black lycra and a screaming orange wig, has attracted an audience before singing a note. An old man, the peak of his cap almost meeting the jut of his chin, has dragged a chair across from the café to sit directly in front of the microphone. As the singer starts her first number, some village boys made bold by his example come out of the shadows to stand by the old man's chair. All of them stare as though hypnotized at the shiny black pelvis rotating just above their heads.

The village girls, short of partners, dance with each other, as close as possible to the backs of the mesmerized boys. One of the waiters puts down his tray to caper in front of a pretty girl sitting with her parents. She blushes and ducks her head, but her mother nudges her to dance. Go on. The holiday will soon be over.

After an hour of music that threatens to dislodge the windows of the houses round the square, the group performs its finale. With an intensity worthy of Piaf on a sad night, the singer gives us *Comme d'habitude*, or My Way, ending with a sob, her orange head bent over the microphone. The old man nods and bangs his stick on the ground, and the dancers go back to the café to see if there's any beer left.

Normally, there would have been *feux d'artifice* shooting up from the field behind the war memorial. This year, because of the drought, fireworks are forbidden. But it was a good *fête*. And did you see how the postman danced?

Arrest That Dog!

A friend in London who occasionally keeps me
informed about subjects of international impor-
tance which might not be reported in *Le
Provençal* sent me a disturbing newspaper clipping. It was taken from *The Times*, and it
revealed an enterprise of unspeakable villainy,
a knife thrust deep into the most sensitive part
of a Frenchman's anatomy.

A gang of scoundrels had been importing
white truffles (sometimes contemptuously
referred to as 'industrial' truffles) from Italy,
and staining them with walnut dye until their
complexions were dark enough to pass as black
truffles. These, as every gourmet knows, have
infinitely more flavour than their white cousins,
and cost infinitely more money. *The Times*
reporter, I think, had seriously underestimated
the prices. He had quoted 400 francs a kilo,
which would have caused a stampede at Fau-
chon in Paris, where I had seen them arranged

in the window like jewels at 7,000 francs a kilo.

But that wasn't the point. It was the nature of the crime that mattered. Here were the French, self-appointed world champions of gastronomy, being taken in by counterfeit delicacies, their taste-buds hoodwinked and their wallets plucked clean. Worse still, the fraud didn't even depend on second-class domestic truffles, but on pallid cast-offs from Italy – *Italy*, for God's sake!

I had once heard a Frenchman express his opinion of Italian food in a single libellous phrase: after the noodle, there is nothing. And yet hundreds, maybe thousands, of dusky Italian impersonators had found their way into knowledgeable French stomachs under the crudest of false pretences. The shame of it was enough to make a man weep all over his *foie gras*.

The story reminded me of Alain, who had offered to take me for a day of truffle hunting below Mont Ventoux, and to demonstrate the skills of his miniature pig. But when I called him, he told me he was having a very thin season, the result of the summer drought. *En* 27 *plus*, the experiment with the pig had been a failure. She was not suited to the work. Nevertheless, he had a few truffles if we were interested, small but good. We arranged to meet in Apt, where he had to see a man about a dog.

There is one café in Apt which is filled, on market day, with men who have truffles to sell. While they wait for customers, they pass the time cheating at cards and lying about how much they were able to charge a passing Parisian for 150 grammes of mud and fungus. They carry folding scales in their pockets, and ancient wooden-handled Opinel knives that are used to cut tiny nicks in the surface of a truffle to prove that its blackness is more than skin-deep. Mixed in with the café smell of coffee and black tobacco is the earthy, almost putrid scent that comes from the contents of the shabby linen bags on the tables. Early morning glasses of *rosé* are sipped, and conversations are often conducted in secretive mutters.

While I waited for Alain, I watched two men crouched over their drinks, their heads close together, glancing around between sentences. One of them took out a cracked Bic pen and wrote something on the palm of his hand. He showed what he had written to the other man and then spat into his palm and carefully rubbed out the evidence. What could it have been? The new price per kilo? The combination of the vault in the bank next door? Or a warning? *Say nothing. A man with glasses is staring at us.*

Alain arrived, and everyone in the café looked at him, as they had looked at me. I felt as though I was about to do something dangerous and illegal instead of buying ingredients for an omelette.

I had brought with me the clipping from *The Times,* but it was old news to Alain. He had heard about it from a friend in the Périgord, where it was causing a great deal of righteous indignation among honest truffle dealers, and grave suspicions in the minds of their customers.

Alain had come to Apt to begin negotiations on the purchase of a new truffle dog. He knew the owner, but not well, and therefore the business would take some time. The asking price was substantial, 20,000 francs, and nothing could be taken on trust. Tests in the field would have to be arranged. The dog's age would have to be established, and his stamina and scenting skills demonstrated. One never knew.

I asked about the miniature pig. Alain shrugged, and drew his index finger across his throat. In the end, he said, unless one was prepared to accept the inconvenience of a full-sized pig, a dog was the only solution. But to find the right dog, a dog that would be worth its weight in banknotes, that was not at all straightforward.

There is no such breed as a truffle hound. Most of the truffle dogs that I had seen were small, nondescript, yappy creatures which looked as though a terrier might have been briefly involved in the bloodline many generations ago. Alain himself had an old Alsatian which, in its day, had worked well. It was all a question of individual instinct and training, and there were no guarantees that a dog who performed for one owner would perform for another. Alain remembered something, and smiled. There was a famous story. I refilled his glass, and he told me.

A man from St Didier once had a dog who could find truffles, so he said, where no other dog had found them before. Throughout the winter, when other hunters were coming back from the hills with a handful, or a dozen, the man from St Didier would return to the café with his satchel bulging. The dog was a *merveille*, and the owner never stopped boasting about his little Napoleon, so called because his nose was worth gold.

Many men coveted Napoleon, but each time they offered to buy him, the owner refused. Until one day, a man came into the café and put four *briques* on the table, four thick wads pinned together, 40,000 francs. This was an extraordinary price and, with a show of reluctance, it was finally accepted. Napoleon went off with his new master.

For the remainder of the season, he didn't find a single truffle. The new owner was *en colère*. He brought Napoleon to the café and demanded his money back. The old owner told him to go away and learn how to hunt properly. Such an *imbécile* didn't deserve a dog like Napoleon. Other unpleasant words were exchanged, 31 but there was no question of the money being refunded.

The new owner went into Avignon to find a lawyer. The lawyer said, as lawyers often do, that it was a grey area. There was no precedent to refer to, no case in the long and meticulously documented history of French law that touched on the matter of a dog being derelict in his duty. It was without doubt a dispute that would have to be decided by a learned judge.

Months and many consultations later, the two men were instructed to appear in court. The judge, being a thorough and conscientious man, wanted to be sure that all the principals in the case were present. A gendarme was sent to arrest the dog and bring him to court as a material witness.

Whether or not the dog's presence in the witness box helped the judge in his deliberations is not known, but he handed down the following verdict: Napoleon was to be returned to his old owner, who would repay half the purchase price, being allowed to keep the other half as compensation for loss of the dog's services.

Now reunited, Napoleon and his old owner moved from St Didier to a village north of Carpentras. Two years later, an identical case was reported, although due to inflation the amount of money had increased. Napoleon and his owner had done it again.

But there was something I didn't understand. If the dog was such a virtuoso truffle hunter, surely his owner would make more money by working him than selling him, even though he ended up keeping the dog and half the money each time he went to court.

Ah, said Alain, you have assumed, like everyone else, that the truffles in the satchel were found by Napoleon on the days they were brought into the café.

Non?

Non. They were kept in the *congélateur* and brought out once or twice a week. That dog couldn't find a pork chop in a *charcuterie*. He had a nose of wood.

Alain finished his wine. 'You must never buy a dog in a café. Only when you have seen him work.' He looked at his watch. 'I have time for another glass. And you?'

Always, I said. Did he have another story?

'This you will like, being a writer,' he said. 'It happened many years ago, but I am told it is true.'

The peasant owned a patch of land some distance from his house. It was not a big patch, less than two *hectares*, but it was crowded with ancient oaks, and each winter there were many truffles, enough to allow the peasant to live in comfortable idleness for the rest of the year. His pig barely needed to search. Year after year, truffles grew more or less where they had grown before. It was like finding money under the trees. God was good, and a prosperous old age was assured.

One can imagine the peasant's irritation the first morning he noticed freshly displaced earth under the tree. Something had been on his land during the night, possibly a dog or even a stray pig. A little further on, he noticed a cigarette end crushed into the earth; a modern, filter-tipped cigarette, not of the kind he smoked. And certainly not dropped by a stray pig. This was extremely alarming.

34   As he went from tree to tree, so his alarm

increased. More earth had been disturbed, and he saw fresh grazes on some rocks that could only have been made by a truffle pick.

It wasn't, it couldn't have been, one of his neighbours. He had known them all since childhood. It must have been a foreigner, someone who didn't know that this precious patch was his.

Since he was a reasonable man, he had to admit that there was no way a foreigner could tell if the land was privately owned or not. Fences and signs were expensive, and he had never seen the need for them. His land was his land; everyone knew that. Clearly, times had changed and strangers were finding their way into the hills. He drove to the nearest town that afternoon and bought an armful of signs: *Propriété privée*, *Défense d'entrer* and, for good measure, three or four that read *Chien méchant*. He and his wife worked until dark nailing them up around the perimeter of the land.

A few days went by without any further signs of the trespasser with the truffle pick, and the peasant allowed himself to relax. It had been an innocent mistake, although he did wonder why an innocent man would hunt truffles at night.

And then it happened again. The signs had been ignored, the land violated and who knows how many fat black nuggets taken from the earth under cover of darkness. It could no longer be excused as the mistake of an ignorant enthusiast. This was a *braconnier*, a poacher, a thief in the night who hoped to profit from an old man's only source of income.

The peasant and his wife discussed the problem that night as they sat in the kitchen and ate their *soupe*. They could, of course, call in the police. But since truffles – or at least, the money made from selling the truffles – did not officially exist, it might not be prudent to involve the authorities. Questions would be asked about the value of what had been stolen, and private information such as this was best kept private. Besides, the official penalty for truffle poaching, even if it were a spell in jail, would not replace the thousands of francs that were even now stuffed in the poacher's deep and dishonest pockets.

And so the couple decided to seek tougher

but more satisfactory justice, and the peasant went to see two of his neighbours, men who would understand what needed to be done.

They agreed to help him, and for several long, cold nights the three of them waited with their shotguns among the truffle oaks, coming home each dawn slightly tipsy from the *marc* that they had been obliged to drink to keep out the chill. At last, one night when clouds scudded across the face of the moon and the Mistral bit into the faces of the three men, they saw the headlights of a car. It stopped at the end of a dirt track, 200 metres down the hill.

The engine stopped, lights were extinguished, doors opened and quietly closed. There were voices, and then the glow of a torch, which came slowly up the hill towards them.

First into the trees was a dog. He stopped, picked up the scent of the men and barked – a high, nervous bark, followed at once by *sssst!* as the poacher hissed him quiet. The men flexed their numb fingers for a better grip of their guns, and the peasant took aim with the torch he had brought specially for the ambush.

The beam caught them as they came into the clearing: a couple, middle-aged and unremarkable, the woman carrying a small sack, the man with torch and truffle pick. Red-handed.

The three men, making great display of their artillery, approached the couple. They had no defence, and with gun barrels under their noses quickly admitted that they had been before to steal truffles.

How many truffles? asked the old peasant. Two kilos? Five kilos? More?

Silence from the poachers, and silence from the three men as they thought about what they should do. Justice must be done; more important than justice, money must be repaid. One of the men whispered in the old peasant's ear, and he nodded. Yes, that is what we will do. He announced the verdict of the impromptu court.

Where was the poacher's bank? Nyons? *Ah bon.* If you start walking now you will be there when it opens. You will take out 30,000 francs, which you will bring back here. We shall keep your car and your dog and your wife until you return.

The poacher set off on the four-hour walk to Nyons. His dog was put in the boot of the car, his wife in the back seat. The three men squeezed in too. It was a cold night. They dozed through it in between tots of *marc*.

Dawn came, then morning, then noon . . .

Alain stopped his story. 'You're a writer,' he said. 'How do you think it ended?'

I made a couple of guesses, both wrong, and Alain laughed.

'It was very simple, not at all *dramatique*,' he said. 'Except perhaps for the wife. The poacher went to his bank in Nyons and took out all the money he possessed, and then – *pouf!* – he disappeared.'

'He never came back?'

'Nobody ever saw him again.'

'Not his wife?'

'Certainly not his wife. He was not fond of his wife.'

'And the peasant?'

'He died an angry man.'

Alain said he had to go. I paid him for the truffles, and wished him luck with his new dog. When I got home, I cut one of the truffles in half to make sure it was the genuine, deep black all the way through. He seemed like a good fellow, Alain, but you never know.

Life Through Rosé-Tinted Spectacles

Going native.

I don't know whether it was meant as a joke, an insult or a compliment, but that was what the man from London said. He had dropped in unexpectedly on his way to the coast, and stayed for lunch. We hadn't seen him for five years, and he was obviously curious to see what effects life in Provence was having on us, examining us thoughtfully for signs of moral and physical deterioration.

We weren't conscious of having changed, but he was sure of it, although there was nothing he could put his finger on. For lack of any single change as plain as delirium tremens, rusty English or premature senility, he put us in the vague, convenient and all-embracing pigeonhole marked 'going native'.

As he drove away in his clean car, telephone antenna fluttering gaily in the breeze, I looked at our small and dusty Citroën, which was 41 innocent of any communications facility. That was certainly a native car. And, in comparison with our visitor's Côte d'Azur outfit, I was wearing native dress – old shirt, shorts, no shoes. Then I remembered how often he had looked at his watch during lunch, because he was meeting friends at Nice at 6.30. Not later in the day, not some time that evening, but at 6.30. Precisely. We had long ago abandoned time-keeping of such a high standard due to lack of local support, and now lived according to the rules of the approximate rendezvous. Another native habit.

The more I thought about it, the more I realized that we must have changed. I wouldn't have called it going native, but there are dozens of differences between our old life and our new life, and we have had to adjust to them. It hasn't been difficult. Most of the changes have taken place gradually, pleasantly, almost impercep-tibly. All of them, I think, are changes for the better.

We no longer watch television. It wasn't a self-righteous decision to give us time for more intellectual pursuits; it simply happened. In the summer, watching television can't begin to compare with watching the evening sky. In the winter, it can't compete with dinner. The television set has now been relegated to a cupboard to make space for more books.

We eat better than we used to, and probably more cheaply. It is impossible to live in France for any length of time and stay immune to the national enthusiasm for food, and who would want to? Why not make a daily pleasure out of a daily necessity? We have slipped into the gastronomic rhythm of Provence, taking advantage of the special offers provided by nature all through the year: asparagus, tiny *haricots verts* barely thicker than matchsticks, fat *fèves*, cherries, aubergines, *courgettes*, peppers, peaches and apricots and melons and grapes, *blette*, wild mushrooms, olives, truffles – every season brings its own treat. With the expensive exception of the truffle, nothing costs more than a few francs a kilo.

Meat is a different matter, and butchers' prices can make the visitor wince. Provence is not cattle country, and so the Englishman in search of his roast beef on Sunday had better 43 take his cheque book and be prepared for disappointment, because the beef is neither cheap nor tender. But lamb, above all from the area round Sisteron where the sheep season themselves with herbs, has a taste that it would be a crime to disguise with mint sauce. And every part of the pig is good.

Even so, we now eat less meat. An occasional *appellation contrôlée* chicken from Bresse, the wild rabbits that Henriette brings in the winter, a *cassoulet* when the temperature drops and the Mistral howls round the house – meat from time to time is wonderful. Meat every day is a habit of the past. There is so much else: fish from the Mediterranean, fresh pasta, limitless recipes for all those vegetables, dozens of breads, hundreds of cheeses.

It may be the change in our diet and the way it is cooked, always in olive oil, but we have both lost weight. Only a little, but enough to cause some surprise to friends who expect us to have developed the ballooning *embonpoint* – the stomach on stilts – that sometimes grows on people with good appetites who have the luck to eat in France.

44

Through no deliberate intention of our own, we also take more exercise. Not the grim contortions promoted by gaunt women in leotards, but the exercise which comes naturally from living in a climate that allows you to spend eight or nine months of the year outdoors. Discipline has nothing to do with it, apart from the small disciplines of country life – bringing logs in for the fire, keeping the weeds down and the ditches clear, planting, pruning, bending and lifting. And, every day in every kind of weather, walking.

We have had people to stay who refuse to believe that walking can be hard exercise. It's not dramatic effort, not immediately punishing, not fast, not violent. Everybody walks, they say. You can't call that exercise. Eventually, if they insist, we take them out for a stroll with the dogs.

For the first ten minutes the going is flat, along the footpath at the bottom of the mountain, easy and undemanding. Pleasant to get a little fresh air and a view of Mont Ventoux in the distance. But exercise? They're not even short of breath.

Then we turn and go up the track leading to the cedar forest that grows along the spine of the Lubéron. The surface changes from sandy soil cushioned with pine needles to rocks and patches of scree, and we begin to climb. After five minutes, there are no more condescending remarks about walking being an old man's exercise. After ten minutes, there are no remarks at all, only the sound of increasingly heavy breathing, punctuated by coughing. The track twists around boulders and under branches so low you have to bend double. There is no encouraging glimpse of the top; the view is limited to a hundred yards or so of narrow, stony, steeply inclined track before it disappears round the next outcrop of rock. If there is any breath to spare, there might be a curse as an ankle turns on the shifting scree. Legs and lungs are burning.

The dogs pad on ahead, with the rest of us strung out behind them at irregular intervals, the least fit stumbling along with their backs bent and their hands on their thighs. Pride usually prevents them from stopping, and they 46 wheeze away stubbornly, heads down, feeling sick. They will never again dismiss walking as non-exercise.

The prize when you reach the top is to find yourself in a silent, extraordinary landscape, sometimes eerie, always beautiful. The cedars are magnificent, and magical when they are draped with great swags of snow. Beyond them, on the south face of the mountain, the land drops away sharply, grey and jagged, softened by the thyme and box that seem to be able to grow in the most unpromising wrinkle of rock.

On a clear day, when the Mistral has blown and the air shines, the views towards the sea are long and sharply focused, almost as if they have been magnified, and there is a sense of being hundreds of miles away from the rest of the world. I once met a peasant up there, on the road the forest service made through the cedars. He was on an old bicycle, a gun slung across his back, a dog loping beside him. We were both startled to see another human being. It is normally less busy, and the only sound is the wind nagging at the trees.

The days pass slowly but the weeks rush by. We now measure the year in ways that have 47 little to do with diaries and specific dates. There is the almond blossom in February, and a few weeks of pre-spring panic in the garden as we try to do the work we've been talking about doing all winter. Spring is a mixture of cherry blossom and a thousand weeds and the first guests of the year, hoping for sub-tropical weather and often getting nothing but rain and wind. Summer might start in April. It might start in May. We know it's arrived when Bernard calls to help us uncover and clean the pool.

Poppies in June, drought in July, storms in August. The vines begin to turn rusty, the hunters come out of their summer hibernation, the grapes have been picked and the water in the pool nips more and more fiercely until it becomes too cold for anything more than a masochistic plunge in the middle of the day. It must be the end of October.

Winter is filled with good resolutions, and some of them are actually achieved. A dead tree is cut down, a wall is built, the old steel garden chairs are repainted, and whenever there is time to spare we take up the dictionary and resume our struggle with the French language.

Our French has improved, and the thought of spending an evening in totally French company is not as daunting as it used to be. But, to use the words that were so often used in my school reports, there is considerable room for improvement. Must try harder. And so we inch our way through books by Pagnol and Giono and de Maupassant, buy *Le Provençal* regularly, listen to the machine-gun delivery of radio news-readers and attempt to unravel the mysteries of what we are constantly being told is a supremely logical language.

I think that is a myth, invented by the French to bewilder foreigners. Where is the logic, for instance, in the genders given to proper names and nouns? Why is the Rhône masculine and the Durance feminine? They are both rivers, and if they must have a sex, why can't it be the same one? When I asked a Frenchman to explain this to me, he delivered a dissertation on sources, streams and floods which, according to him, answered the question conclusively and, of course, logically. Then he went on to the masculine ocean, the feminine sea, the masculine lake and the feminine puddle. Even the water must get confused.

His speech did nothing to change my theory, which is that genders are there for no other reason than to make life difficult. They have been allocated in a whimsical and arbitrary fashion, sometimes with a cavalier disregard for the anatomical niceties. The French for vagina is *vagin*. *Le vagin*. Masculine. How can the puzzled student hope to apply logic to a language in which the vagina is masculine?

There is also the androgynous *lui* waiting to ambush us at the threshold of many a sentence. Normally, *lui* is him. In some constructions, *lui* is her. Often, we are left in the dark as to *lui*'s gender until it is made known to us some time after he or she has been introduced, as in: '*Je lui ai appelé*' (I called him), '*mais elle était occupée*' (but she was busy). A short-lived mystery, possibly, but one which can trip up the novice, particularly when *lui*'s first name is also a mixture of masculine and feminine, such as Jean-Marie or Marie-Pierre.

And that is not the worst of it. Strange and
unnatural events take place every day within

the formalities of French syntax. A recent newspaper article, reporting on the marriage of the rock singer Johnny Halliday, paused in its description of the bride's frock to give Johnny a pat on the back. '*Il est*,' said the article, '*une grande vedette*.' In the space of a single short sentence, the star had undergone a sex change, and on his wedding day too.

It is perhaps because of these perplexing twists and turns that French was for centuries the language of diplomacy, an occupation in which simplicity and clarity are not regarded as being necessary, or even desirable. Indeed, the guarded statement, made fuzzy by formality and open to several different interpretations, is much less likely to land an ambassador in the soup than plain words which mean what they say. A diplomat, according to Alex Dreier, is 'anyone who thinks twice before saying nothing'. Nuance and significant vagueness are essential, and French might have been invented to allow these linguistic weeds to flourish in the crevices of every sentence.

But it is a beautiful, supple and romantic language, although it may not quite deserve the reverence that inspires a course of French lessons to be described as a '*cours de civilisation*' by those who regard it as a national treasure and a shining example of how everyone should speak. One can imagine the dismay of these purists at the foreign horrors that are now creeping into everyday French.

The rot probably started when *le weekend* slipped across the Channel to Paris at about the same time that a nightclub owner in Pigalle christened his establishment *Le Sexy*. Inevitably, this led to the naughty institution of *le weekend sexy*, to the delight of Parisian hotel owners and the despair of their counterparts in Brighton and other less erotically blessed resorts.

The invasion of the language hasn't stopped in the bedroom. It has also infiltrated the office. The executive now has *un job*. If the pressure of work becomes too much for him, he will find himself increasingly *stressé*, perhaps because of the demands of being *un leader* in the business jungle of *le marketing*. The poor, overworked wretch doesn't even have time for the traditional three-hour lunch, and has to make do with *le fast-food*. It is the worst kind of Franglais, and it goads the elders of the Académie Française into fits of outrage. I can't say I blame them. These clumsy intrusions into such a graceful language are *scandaleux*; or, to put it another way, *les pits*.

The gradual spread of Franglais is helped by the fact that there are many fewer words in the French vocabulary than in English. This has its own set of problems, because the same word can have more than one meaning. In Paris, for instance, *'je suis ravi'* will normally be taken to mean 'I am delighted.' In the Café du Progrès in Ménerbes, however, *ravi* has a second, uncomplimentary translation, and the same phrase can mean 'I am the village idiot.'

In order to disguise my confusion and to avoid at least some of the many verbal booby-traps, I have learned to grunt like a native, to make those short but expressive sounds – those sharp intakes of breath, those understanding clickings of the tongue, those mutters of *beh oui* – that are used like conversational stepping stones in between one subject and the next.

Of all these, the most flexible and therefore 53

most useful is the short and apparently explicit phrase *ah bon*, used with or without a question mark. I used to think this meant what it said, but of course it doesn't. A typical exchange, with the right degree of catastrophe and gloom, might go something like this:

'Young Jean-Pierre is in real trouble this time.'

'*Oui?*'

'*Beh oui.* He came out of the café, got in his car, ran over a *gendarme* – completely *écrasé* – drove into a wall, went through the windscreen, split his head open and broke his leg in fourteen places.'

'*Ah bon.*'

Depending on inflection, *ah bon* can express shock, disbelief, indifference, irritation or joy – a remarkable achievement for two short words.

Similarly, it is possible to conduct the greater part of a brief conversation with two other monosyllables – *ça va* – which means literally 'it goes'. Every day, in every town and village around Provence, acquaintances will meet on the street, perform the ritual handshake and deliver the ritual dialogue:

54   '*Cça va?*'

'*Oui. Ça va, ça va. Et vous?*'
'*Bohf, ça va.*'
'*Bieng. Ça va alors.*'
'*Oui, oui. Ça va.*'
'*Allez. Au 'voir.*'
'*Au 'voir.*'

The words alone do not do justice to the occasion, which is decorated with shrugs and sighs and thoughtful pauses that can stretch to two or three minutes if the sun is shining and there is nothing pressing to do. And, naturally, the same unhurried, pleasant acknowledgement of neighbourhood faces will be repeated several times in the course of the morning's errands.

It is easy to be misled, after a few months of these uncomplicated encounters, into believing that you are beginning to distinguish yourself in colloquial French. You may even have spent long evenings with French people who profess to understand you. They become more than acquaintances; they become friends. And when they judge the moment is ripe, they present you with the gift of friendship in spoken form, which brings with it an entirely new set of opportunities to make a fool of yourself. Instead 55 of using *vous*, they will start addressing you as *tu* or *toi*, a form of intimacy that has its own verb, *tutoyer*.

The day when a Frenchman switches from the formality of *vous* to the familiarity of *tu* is a day to be taken seriously. It is an unmistakable signal that he has decided – after weeks or months or sometimes years – that he likes you. It would be churlish and unfriendly of you not to return the compliment. And so, just when you are at last feeling reasonably comfortable with *vous* and all the plurals that go with it, you are thrust headlong into the singular world of *tu*. (Unless of course, you follow the example of ex-President Giscard d'Estaing, who apparently addresses even his wife as *vous*.)

But we stumble along, committing all kinds of sins against grammar and gender, making long and awkward detours to avoid the swamps of the subjunctive and the chasms in our vocabularies, hoping that our friends are not too appalled at the mauling we give their language. They are kind enough to say that our French doesn't make them shudder. I doubt that, but there is no doubting their desire to help us feel at home, and there is a warmth to everyday life that is not just the sun.

That, at least, has been our experience. It obviously isn't universal, and some people either don't believe it, or even seem to resent it. We have been accused of the crime of cheerfulness, of turning a blind eye to minor problems, and of deliberately ignoring what is invariably described as the dark side of the Provençal character. This ominous cliché is wheeled out and festooned with words like dishonest, lazy, bigoted, greedy and brutal. It is as if they are peculiarly local characteristics which the innocent foreigner – honest, industrious, unprejudiced and generally blameless – will be exposed to for the first time in his life.

It is of course true that there are crooks and bigots in Provence, just as there are crooks and bigots everywhere. But we've been lucky, and Provence has been good to us. We will never be more than permanent visitors in someone else's country, but we have been made welcome and happy. There are no regrets, few complaints, many pleasures.

Merci Provence.

PENGUIN 60S

ISABEL ALLENDE · *Voices in My Ear*
NICHOLSON BAKER · *Playing Trombone*
LINDSEY BAREHAM · *The Little Book of Big Soups*
KAREN BLIXEN · *From the Ngong Hills*
DIRK BOGARDE · *Coming of Age*
ANTHONY BURGESS · *Childhood*
ANGELA CARTER · *Lizzie Borden*
CARLOS CASTANEDA · *The Sorcerer's Ring of Power*
ELIZABETH DAVID · *Peperonata and Other Italian Dishes*
RICHARD DAWKINS · *The Pocket Watchmaker*
GERALD DURRELL · *The Pageant of Fireflies*
RICHARD ELLMANN · *The Trial of Oscar Wilde*
EPICURUS · *Letter on Happiness*
MARIANNE FAITHFULL · *Year One*
KEITH FLOYD · *Hot and Spicy Floyd*
ALEXANDER FRATER · *Where the Dawn Comes Up like Thunder*
ESTHER FREUD · *Meeting Bilal*
JOHN KENNETH GALBRAITH · *The Culture of Contentment*
ROB GRANT AND DOUG NAYLOR · *Scenes from the Dwarf*
ROBERT GRAVES · *The Gods of Olympus*
JANE GRIGSON · *Puddings*
SOPHIE GRIGSON · *From Sophie's Table*
KATHARINE HEPBURN · *Little Me*
JAMES HERRIOT · *Seven Yorkshire Tales*
SUSAN HILL · *The Badness within Him*
ALAN HOLLINGHURST · *Adventures Underground*
BARRY HUMPHRIES · *Less is More Please*
HOWARD JACOBSON · *Expulsion from Paradise*
P. D. JAMES · *The Girl Who Loved Graveyards*
STEPHEN KING · *Umney's Last Case*

PENGUIN 60s

READ MORE IN PENGUIN

For complete information about books available from Penguin and how to order them, please write to us at the appropriate address below. Please note that for copyright reasons the selection of books varies from country to country.

IN THE UNITED KINGDOM: Please write to *Dept. EP, Penguin Books Ltd, Bath Road, Harmondsworth, Middlesex UB7 0DA*.

IN THE UNITED STATES: Please write to *Consumer Sales, Penguin USA, P.O. Box 999, Dept. 17109, Bergenfield, New Jersey 07621-0120*. VISA and MasterCard holders call 1-800-253-6476 to order Penguin titles.

IN CANADA: Please write to *Penguin Books Canada Ltd, 10 Alcorn Avenue, Suite 300, Toronto, Ontario M4V 3B2*.

IN AUSTRALIA: Please write to *Penguin Books Australia Ltd, P.O. Box 257, Ringwood, Victoria 3134*.

IN NEW ZEALAND: Please write to *Penguin Books (NZ) Ltd, Private Bag 102902, North Shore Mail Centre, Auckland 10*.

IN INDIA: Please write to *Penguin Books India Pvt Ltd, 706 Eros Apartments, 56 Nehru Place, New Delhi 110 019*.

IN THE NETHERLANDS: Please write to *Penguin Books Netherlands bv, Postbus 3507, NL-1001 AH Amsterdam*.

IN GERMANY: Please write to *Penguin Books Deutschland GmbH, Metzlerstrasse 26, 60594 Frankfurt am Main*.

IN SPAIN: Please write to *Penguin Books S. A., Bravo Murillo 19, 1° B, 28015 Madrid*.

IN ITALY: Please write to *Penguin Italia s.r.l., Via Felice Casati 20, I-20124 Milano*.

IN FRANCE: Please write to *Penguin France S. A., 17 rue Lejeune, F-31000 Toulouse*.

IN JAPAN: Please write to *Penguin Books Japan, Ishikiribashi Building, 2-5-4, Suido, Bunkyo-ku, Tokyo 112*.

IN GREECE: Please write to *Penguin Hellas Ltd, Dimocritou 3, GR-106 71 Athens*.

IN SOUTH AFRICA: Please write to *Longman Penguin Southern Africa (Pty) Ltd, Private Bag X08, Bertsham 2013*.